MW01701435

Self Published 2025 by Anna Marie Burdette in cooperation with
Dragonfly Rose | DragonflyRose.com/Love
All Photos and art were created by Anna Marie Burdette

Publisher Dragonfly Rose
ISBN: 979-8-9923985-0-2

Copyright January 18th 2025
Special Edition: Hard cover binding and high quality print images
Collectors Version
First Edition 2025

Going BareFoot

A Collection of Poetic Reflections, Art, and Photography

by Anna Marie B.

VOL. I

Copyright © 2025 Anna Marie Burdette | Dragonfly Rose

This is my first book and it would still be sitting on my hard drive, unfinished, without the love and support from Aaron Hall. Thank you for your help in editing and listening, your insight, and most of all for loving and accepting every part of me. I hope my love inspires you, the way your love inspires me. You are my Moon and Stars. I love you.

TABLE OF CONTENTS

ANNA MARIE

I thank you for giving of your own time today, on this journey through life, to read my words. There are many pieces to who I am as a person and the challenges I have had to overcome thus far. This is my poetic attempt to unravel my emotions and the ways in which I have healed from my traumas, and how I am stepping out of my survival mind and into being fully who I am, one barefoot step at a time. Learning to live authentically upon this planet.

One big lesson I have learned is this:
Life happens and it can be undeniably hard at times. We choose how we respond to the events that unfold in our lives. Sometimes we develop survival skills that we have to unlearn as adults. But, as with any journey, we must first take off our shoes and walk through our souls, letting ourselves feel everything so we can heal, so we can get to know ourselves, and so we can live authentically as who we are.

How To Use This Book:

The pages to come house deep parts of my soul portrayed in poetic form. Some of my reflections will have an accompanying explanation centering on what I was going through and how I overcame the feelings that I am writing about.

Sometimes great breakthroughs can happen for us with a simple question. I have included questions for you to journal and reflect on your own experiences so you can heal and walk proudly, fully embracing all that you are, in every moment.

You are the one relationship that you can never escape, so make it the best one!

There are also poems included in this book that reflect my thoughts and feelings about our world and our place in it.

Art and photography have played vital roles in my healing journey. I have included some of my work in the pages to come. Many are available as prints if you would like one for your wall. You can inquire about any of my pieces through email at Anna@DragonflyRose.com

The art, photography, and poems span from 2010 to 2024

Gypsy Soul

Like moths to a flame they come, whirling toward me,
Like the waters of a rolling rapid on the brink
Of a falling curtain of water.
My dreams overwhelm my mind, my body, my soul, and spirit.
I feel the breeze and I have a pull
To flow wherever it happens to be blowing,
To be a gypsy traveling on the tail of the wind.
I gaze upon the cloud-filled sky
And see a bird soaring the heavens,
Its freedom beckons to me,
Whispering the dreams that I buried years ago.
Like sky nymphs, they tease and tantalize my senses,
Reminding me of what it truly means
To be living on this planet.
We are not meant to be prisoners
Of these concrete towers that house
The many things that occupy our wasting time.
The dragon guarding our sky-scraping tower
Is fear in our minds,
And we are our own knights in shining armor.

I hope my words and thoughts help to open new doorways for you, and that you have the courage to step through them.

Tiny Hands

Tiny hands
Trying to grasp big roles.
Good girls are seen,
But never heard.
Why is she mad?
What did I do?

A child
Responsible for a child.
Punished harshly
For making a mistake.

Painful words
Become my psyche,
Become my inner voice.
This is who I am,
I am wrong.

How can I make myself right?
I just want her to hold me,
I just want her to love me,
I just want to feel right and whole,
I want to feel safe in this world.

I became a girl
That hid in the dark,
That hated all she was.
I hid myself away,
Where no one could find me.
Not even me.

Child Abuse

As a child all I wanted was to know was that I was loved. That what I did and said was valid. For my mother to be proud. I did not grow up knowing I was loved by my parents. My mother instilled words of hatred into my views of who I was. These views are still something I struggle with to this day. The words we tell our children (especially the ages birth to 5) is what becomes the words that they think about themselves. It becomes their inner voice. I grew up thinking I was nasty, stupid, an idiot, a Pollock Indian, a slut, a heathen, etc. I had to rewire my brain to overcome this trauma as an adult. These words operated in the background of my psyche and were the foundation for my decisions. They were also the reason I felt like I didn't deserve anything good (love, security, life events, etc.) even though I never did anything to prompt such a feeling.

Some Questions For You:

- What words were instilled into you as a child?
- Do you feel loved?
- What are you hiding from everyone?
- Do you feel like you deserve all the good things in this life?

DISCONSOLATE

A bound mouth,
Words sliding back down my throat,
Laying bricks in the endless pit of my stomach.

I rip open,
For a brief moment,
Like the stitches of a bloated wound.

I lose control;
My words escape
And my feelings pour out.

Hot as lava.
My emotions burn
As I try to express my pain.

But spears always stab slowly and skillfully
Into my heart;
In the form of words and actions.

I am wrong,
For feeling,
For everything.

No feelings are allowed.
Except what serves
Someone else's ego

I retreat into the depths,
Into the darkness of my soul,
I am disconsolate.

Hopeless and fundamentally flawed.

Feelings of Wrong'ness

Disconsolate is feeling deep sadness or despair, often accompanied by a sense of hopelessness or feeling fundamentally flawed.

My entire life, I have been taught I was flawed or wrong. Wrong in what I say, what I do, and wrong in what I feel. This left me in spaces of intense self-hatred and self-doubt. I didn't trust myself, and I didn't like who I was. I felt like I was wrong, like no matter what I did I couldn't get anything right. These feelings caused me to hurt myself when I was in my teens; it caused me to seek out abusive partners; it caused me to feel like I was an alien among all other humans. It caused me to retreat so deep into myself that I could no longer find myself. It wasn't until I had gotten so low that I wanted to die that I pulled myself up and out. My kids saved me; I couldn't abandon them like that. I had to protect them the way I was never protected. I made drastic changes and started facing myself. I had to show those parts of my soul that I could be trusted. That trust took many years, and the biggest part of that trust came from embracing myself with love, and not judgment.

Some Questions For You:

- Are you able to express what you are feeling freely?
- Do you trust yourself?
- Are you a close friend to yourself?
- Is there anyone in your life that you don't feel safe to express your feelings around?
- Are there any areas that you could shift to live more authentically?
- What in your life needs drastic change?

Encroach

Hands glide and slide
Into seen and unseen places
Without permission.

I've been taught that
This is forgivable,
That I must obey,
That my body
Is not my own.

Because of this
I couldn't see
The damage
I was doing to myself

Lack of healthy boundaries;
Empty and used.
I started saying no.

I had to be okay saying goodbye
To those who used me,
Had to say goodbye
To being a victim.

I embraced myself,
And in doing so,
I filled the abyss within my soul
With Love and found that was
Where my heart was always hiding.

My Body

Men have touched my body without my permission for as long as I can remember. Sometimes I didn't mind, other times it made me uncomfortable. But I was brought up to do what I was told and this included the actions from men towards my body. I had never set boundaries around my body and how I wanted the world to interact with it. It was something that never came into my mind. I would just let it happen and move on. But what I was teaching myself was that people could use my body how they wanted to, even within "friendships". I was teaching myself that my body was for everyone but me. This created relationships where I felt used because I was only wanted for sex, and friendships that were too 'friendly'. It created a void in my heart that felt like the depths of the abyss. In those depths my heart hid away. I felt like a shell of a person. I felt alone. What I had to see was how I was letting people interact with me. I had to see how every action I was taking in every moment determined how the world would interact with me. I had to see how much I was disrespecting myself. I had to learn to love all that I am and to let that be the acceptance I needed. My need for people to accept me turned me into an empty shell. My setting of boundaries started me on the path of healing and self-love. I had to learn to respect my body if I wanted others too.

Some Questions For You:

- What boundaries do you have in place for how others interact with your body?
- Do you respect your own body?
- Do you love your body?
- Do you take care of your body?

Young Mom

Legs in the air,
Unaware
Of what was truly happening,
Feeling nothing but the alcohol
Coursing through my body.

I became
A young mom,
A child having a child,
Grasping for support
Wherever it could be found.

Trying so hard not to damage,
In the ways in which I was damaged.
But where abuse never escaped my hands,
Abuse from others I allowed in did.

Like an inevitable karmic stain
That passed from me onto my children.
My son got an unhealed version of me,
My daughter got a mom healing.

I often wish
I could give my son
What I am giving my daughter.
But I was a young mom,
And I gave what I could

I gave
From a young
and wounded version of myself.

My Mom Guilt

Rape is a word I don't like associating with myself, but I also don't like calling myself a victim. Perhaps that's why it's hard for me to face that this is my reality. My experience wasn't violent, and for that I feel lucky; in fact, I honestly didn't even realize I was having sex.

When I was younger, I was drawn to the idea of having a baby. A child who would love me unconditionally. I love my children with an intense passion, and I would protect them with the same ferocity as a bear guarding her cubs. Yet, despite this fierce love, I never really wanted to have children. But the Universe had other plans for me, or maybe my soul chose this path. However you view it, I became a young mom.

I didn't have a good example of what a mother should be. All I knew was what I didn't want to be. I didn't want to be like my own mother, and that was a starting point. However, even though I never abused my children, others I allowed into our lives did. When I realized it was happening, I would leave immediately. But it became a pattern I couldn't seem to escape, not until I was in my mid-30s to early 40s. It's a painful truth I have to face: no matter what I do, I can't protect them from suffering the same traumas I endured as a child. This thought brings me great sadness and anger.

I do forgive the young mother I was, but I also see how hard I am on myself as an older mother. I'm learning to give myself grace, to stop living in a constant state of worry and anxiety. I am allowing myself to grieve the fact that I never wanted children and the guilt that comes with that. I am grateful to be the mother of my children, but sometimes I feel like I lack the proper tools to be the great mom they deserve.

Some Questions For You:

- Where in your life are you the hardest on yourself?
- Where in your life do you hold guilt?
- Can you forgive yourself?

Empty Explanations

I wish I could explain
How much anger and frustration hurt me,
How it breaks me down into a hollow shell of a being,
How it turns my heart black.

I wish I could explain
The way my heart breaks
When my children don't want me around,
Or my very presence seems to annoy them.

I wish I could explain.

I wish they could see

I wish they could feel through my heart and soul.

There is more anger and frustration here
Than love at times,
And it is too heavy to carry.

I wish I could explain
How the years of trying to make everyone happy,
Every single day,
Has worn me to the point of unhappiness.

I wish I could explain
That I know it is of my own doing.

But the explanations have become exhausting,
I am so fatigued,
And I have been reduced
To nothing more than this hollow empty shell.

Anxious Attachment

I feel
Like I am a person that
Needs to be alone.

Away from
Every energy
Except my own.

But I can't say no
When people want
My time.

My fear of losing them
Outweighs anything
I may want or need for myself.

My fear of losing people
Makes me throw away
whatever I want,
Or dream for myself.

I have been learning to breathe,
To sit with the uncomfortable
Feelings of loss.

I have been learning to be okay
With loss,
Especially when choosing myself.

Those who stay
Are the ones who
Truly love
And respect me.

Those who stay
Are the ones who
Truly know
And care for me.

I need to remember this.

Being Happy Alone

A friend once told me that I need to be happy and complete on my own, so I don't rely on friends or lovers to fill any voids. This made me reflect on how much energy I was putting into finding people to fill that emptiness. I realized that the reason I kept attracting hurtful people was because well-balanced and healthy individuals understand that everything they need is already within themselves. They know that no one outside of them can fill any void they might feel.

I came to see that I needed to be happy alone so I wouldn't keep searching for friendships or partners to complete me. This shift would prevent me from feeling left out or upset when others chose to do things without me. It would also help me set healthier boundaries in my relationships.

SOME QUESTIONS FOR YOU:

- Do you get sad or upset when people want to do things without you?
- Do you feel happy and complete alone?

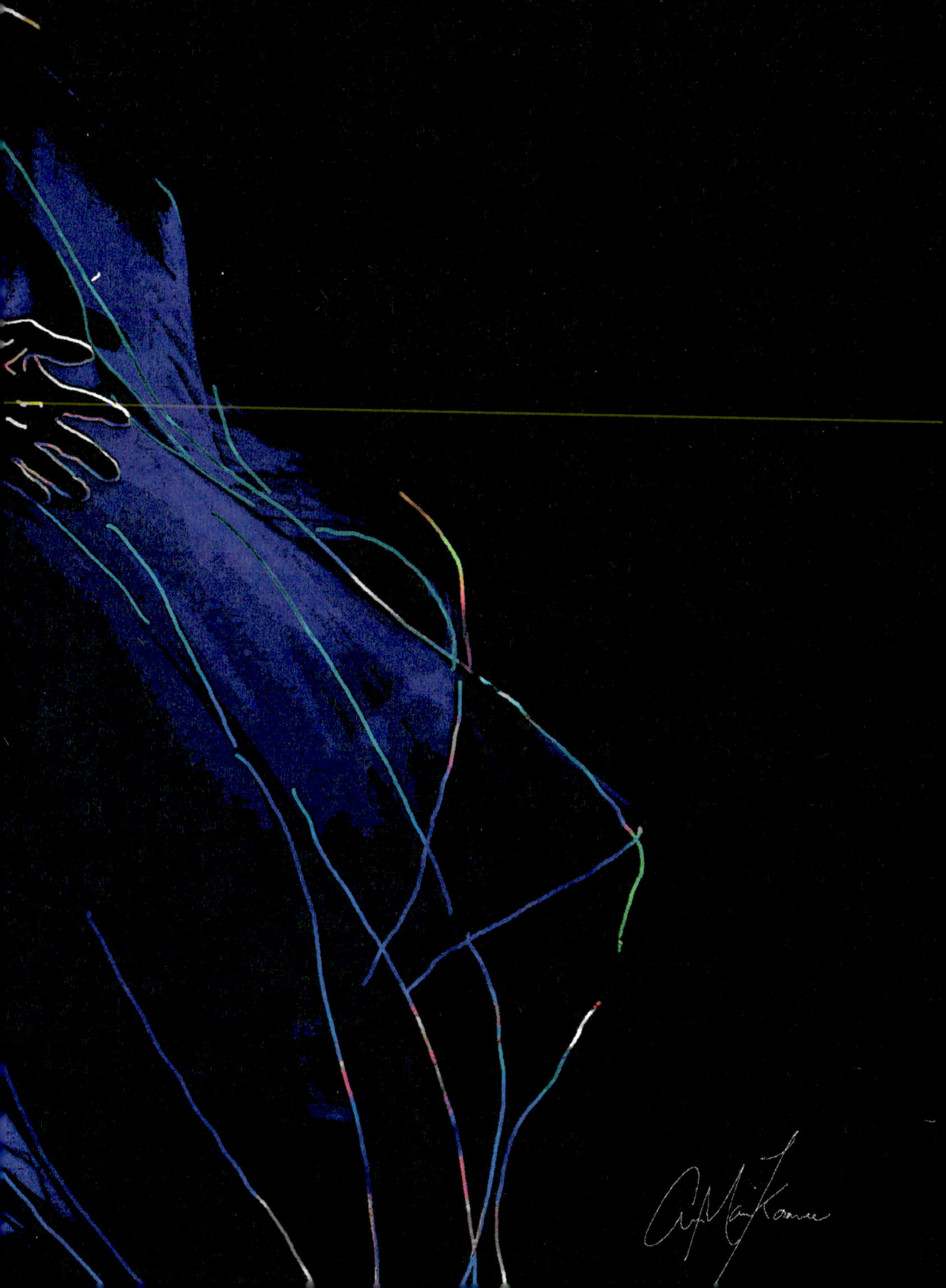

I Am Lake Natron

Lake Natron is a salt, or alkaline, lake located in north Ngorongoro District of Arusha Region in Tanzania at the border with Kenya. The high concentration of natron gives the lake extreme alkaline levels, and it is one of the deadliest lakes on the planet.

I am being swallowed,
Consumed,
By a blackness I cannot escape.

I feel it hanging heavily
From every limb,
Every organ of my body.

I am Lake Natron,
A beautifully deadly water,
Turning you into a calcified corpse.

Maybe
I myself
Am just that.

Where Medusa's stare once held me,
I now float through life,
a lifeless statue.

I know so many methods,
Have so many tools,
To help me escape this.

But I am trapped,
Trapped by the black tar
That holds me.

I don't expect you
To understand,
Because you never will.

You cannot walk in my shoes,
You would never survive
The maze of my mind.

But I don't blame you,
I don't hate you,
Even though at times I do.

Even when good things happen,
The joy within me
Is temporary.

It fades,
Like the moon fades
From a clouded sky.

I am stuck in a loop.
A hallway that continues
Forever with no doors.

You will never
understand me,
This is where love dies.

I cannot be
What you want me
To be…

Soul Fire

There is an angry fire
In my soul.

An inferno
Raging with demons.

Who are trying
To make a home within me.

I am not a vessel
To fill their wounded needs.

I have given my power away
To things,
To people,
to men,
That only fuel my ire.

Instead of providing
Myself a safe space.

A space that fuels
My passions and love.

My heart has retreated,
It has numbed.

Only a shell now remains,
And it is full of primal emotions.

Burning Bridges

In my search for love, I consistently found myself in a space of emptiness. I kept attracting people—including friends—who wanted to use me in some way. Men were often only interested in my body, even if they claimed to be just friends. And friends who appreciated my advice and company but would never include me in any plans. I felt alone and left out. Sometimes people would go many months without ever reaching out or responding. With men I loved sex, but I craved a real connection. A partnership. Someone who wanted to explore every facet of my mind and soul.

Eventually, I realized I had to start saying no and walking away from anyone who didn't align with what I truly wanted. The same went for friendships. I longed for deep, meaningful connections, but the people I tried to connect with would disappear as soon as they were done venting about their lives or when I set firm boundaries around inappropriate messages and touching. I felt like a free counselor, offering help without receiving any benefit in return. And I felt used by people who called themselves friends.

This dynamic fueled a deep anger that, in hindsight, I realize I needed. It gave me the strength to set healthier boundaries and the courage to walk away from anyone who violated them—or disregarded my morals and ethics. I finally became okay with burning some bridges and with truly enjoying being alone.

Some Questions For You:

- Do you feel like an empty shell? If so, what can you do in this very moment to give to yourself?
- Do you feel like the relationships in your life are healthy and balanced?
- Do you feel like you are valued for all the you encompass? Body, mind, and soul?
- Do you value yourself?
- Are you able to walk away from toxic people in your life?

Savage Woman

I used to be a nice,
Quiet
Obedient girl.
My moments
Of rage
Would escape.

I would be
"Put back in my place."
By those
Who feared my power.

I became
Watered down.

Be less,
Smile more,
Cry less.
Too fat,
Too cranky,
Too moody,
Too emotional,
Too loud,
Too crazy.

I watered down
For those who could not hold
The woman I truly am.

I used to be sweet,
Quiet,
Obedient.
People turned me
Into a savage woman.

This life
Has awakened a beast in me
That no longer
Cares to be caged,
No longer cares
To please people.

The love I feel for myself
Has set me free,
The unconditional love
I do receive
Has given me wings.

The truth is
That I am no cup of tea;
I am a shot of tequila.
I will rock your world
In the best way possible,
But watering down
Is something that
I can never do again.

You take me straight up,
With a lick of salt
And a twist of lime.

Warrior

I used to call myself a warrior,
As a term of endearment.
Like it was some sort of admirable accomplishment.

I would fight for anything I deemed worthy.
But as I become older,
I see the damaging effects
Of what being a warrior truly is.

I can't help but think of a real soldier,
And the trauma they experience fighting battles.
How it changes them into something else.

I see this warrior aspect differently now.
It has transformed me into something
That cannot relate to most people.

People that have overcome astronomical challenges,
And have scars in places no one can see,
But remain pure-hearted and kind
Are the people I relate to now.

I now look on that warrior part of myself
And it brings me to tears that I ever
Had to show up in this way.

It has brought me great sorrow,
But also a greater understanding.
Now all being a warrior means
Is that I have gone through trauma.

Wood Nymph

The forest beckons to me
To enter the trailing sunlight.
To dance between
The spaces in the trees.
To lay my head
On a bed of moss,
My hair becoming the soft green I lie upon.

Trees speak to me
In a language
That I understand more clearly
Than any human voice.

I feel the wings upon my back
Dancing to a rhythm that only Mother can beat.
I crave adventures upon her terrain.
The lowest valleys
And the highest mountains.
Peaceful lakes
And raging rivers.

My heart and soul
Are free
In these oasis places.
I was a Wood Nymph
In a past life.

Restless Gypsy Soul

The stars and moon
Fall from the heavens
And collide like meteors
Falling to their graves upon the earth.

As the sun and moon cannot be held,
Neither can I.
I feel like a bird fighting
So her wings will not be clipped.

A city of smog and dirt holds me.
People's expectations of what I should do
And how I should be
Overwhelm my thinning patience.

Life is but a series
Of chance encounters
And lost loves.

Yet in the weighing hours
That the full moon
Pulls on the waters of the ocean,
I want nothing more but to be sailing
The waves of the wind,
And dancing in the flow of life.

Perhaps commitment to anything
Is what I am running from,
Or perhaps it is because I truly believe
That people are only meant to be in our lives
For a short time.

When I sit and search my soul,
I find that I do not want
To 'grow old' with someone.
I just want to be alone.
But perhaps this is yet another
Fleeting emotion
Brought on by exhaustion,
And my overwhelming fear of cages.

I don't think that I will ever want
To truly 'belong' somewhere.

My restless Gypsy Soul.

My Acheron

She walked
With a fire in her soul
And a sadness
In her heart

A love
Emanated from her
Like the powerful light
Of a full moon

She could bring peace
With her presence
But those who hated themselves
Also hated her

This only added
To the Acheron
Of her swallowing
Sadness.

She needed to learn
How to walk away
And how to thrive
Alone.

We Become Our Circle

The Acheron is a river in the NW area of Greece that was once thought to lead to the underworld. Spiritually the Acheron symbolizes woe and misery.

I have always been drawn to those who hate themselves. I see the potential in people and think, "If I just pour into them, they will strive to become the best version of themselves." It took years of heartache for me to realize that just because I can see someone's potential it doesn't mean they will ever reach it, no matter what I do to help.

I had to learn to walk away, and I walked away from many people, including some I considered very close friends. Being alone no longer fills me with anxiety, emptiness, or sadness as it once did. Now, when I am alone, I find my strength and power. One big lesson I have learned over this last year is that who we surround ourselves with determines who we become. By saying no to certain people I changed my energy to attract people who are balanced and will help me grow. The people that once brought me down will become less and less in my life.

We become the energy we think and surround ourselves with. Say no to what you don't want your life to be, and say yes to everything that you do want your life to look like. It may be hard to to at times, but the reward outweighs every cost. I can promise you that.

__Some Questions For You:__

- How do you feel when you are alone?
- Do you tend to surround yourself with people who are balanced? Or unbalanced?
- Would you say that the people in your circle are happy and love who they are?
- Would you say that you are happy and love all that you are?

Within My Darkness

I had to take a seat
Within the dark spaces of my soul

I let the cloak of the cool void
Fold around me

Until even my body
Was gone

Floating as the darkness,
A pure nothingness

From that nothingness
Anything can be created

I began looking at
All the past versions of myself

Each one emerging
From all the dark edges of my mind

Each one unfolding
And expanding

As I embraced each
With unconditional love.

EMBRACING EVERY VERSION

To fully love all that we are, we must first uncover the parts of ourselves that are hiding. We need to go inward and allow the pieces of ourselves we've tucked away to emerge. When this happens, we might experience feelings of 'wrongness' from what originally caused us to shun those aspects of who we are.

We must feel these emotions, embrace them, and forgive ourselves. Relax into each part of who we are and offer ourselves the love and acceptance we deserve, and have been looking for.

To be fully who we are, we must accept ourselves with open arms and unconditional love. By doing this we also strengthen the trust we have within ourselves.

What does this mean? For me it was not pushing away the feelings that society labels as unsavory. There are lessons and healing that lies in the emotions of sorrow, anger, hatred, boredom, etc. For me the "always choose happiness" trend in psychology and 'self-help' was more detrimental than actually feeling through whatever I was feeling. I think this is a toxic form of positivity. We cannot simply fake it, especially if there are deep rooted things that we need to face and heal.

When I am feeling sad, I feel sad. I sit with that feeling. I will dive deep into it and let it consume me. I remember the first time I did this. At first, it was terrifying, but that feeling of fear was overtaken by an image of myself hiding deep within my soul. Curled up, afraid. The part of me that consoles others, the part of me that is a mother, stepped out. I gave myself what I needed most to heal.

I do this with every emotion I experience.

An Exercise For You:

This exercise will help you embrace all versions of yourself, if you choose to do so.

Sit or lie down in a comfortable position.
Close your eyes and begin counting your breath:
In for 4, out for 4.
In for 5, out for 5.
In for 6, out for 6.
In for 7, out for 7.

I find that around 7, I start to release and relax. As you breathe, pull the air from your throat (not your nose). I say "throat" because that is what it feels like. The air traveling through will create a different sound than when pulling air through your nose. But in reality you are breathing through your diaphragm.

Once you are calm and relaxed from breathing, focus on whatever emotion arises. It could be happiness, sadness, anger, frustration, etc. Do not try to shift to a different emotion. Let the emotion fill every inch of your body and soul. If you need to cry, cry. If you need to smile or laugh, do so. You will see yourself in your mind's eye. You may be old, young, or look completely different. Embrace whatever version of yourself comes through. You may interact with yourself in many different ways. Whichever way your inner self is trying to teach you, let it happen.

Once you are finished, open your eyes and journal your experience. Remember to always reflect on your journeys inward. I don't want to place any imprints on your journey, but I also don't want you to be concerned if the encounter isn't what you expected. Every version of myself I have encountered has interacted with me in very different ways. Some are kind and caring, some need to be embraced or hugged, and some try to destroy me in some way. Remember, this too is a journey and you must release control so it can happen. It is a release so we can fully step into who we are. Sometimes we need to be torn down so we can be reborn from whatever remains, like a Phoenix rising from its ashes.

I Welcome This Storm

I feel a pivot happening in my bones,
Change swirling around me,
Like I am in the eye of a hurricane.
I do not fear this storm.
I welcome it.
I understand that to step into a new life,
A new way of being,
To step into myself,
This requires a massive destruction.
I feel the edges of this storm closing in on me,
And I welcome it.
I call it.
Today I was walking down a hall of memories.
I could see myself in pictures over the last 4 years.
Each day I grew dimmer than the day before.
As I stared at a photo of me last year
I saw only a shadow,
A watered down version of who I am.
This storm will destroy,
But I am the master builder of my life.
I look forward to laying new foundations.
To building a castle,
A Taj Mahal of a life.
Yes, I welcome this storm.

How To: Unconditional Self-Love

Frustration streaming down my cheeks,
An inner eruption of emotion,
A hot and steady flow.

"You need to love yourself," Divinity whispered
But how do I do that?
"My sweet child, how do you fall in love with another?"

Every dark corner,
Every doubt,
Every confusion,
Illuminated with one question.

For you fall in love with yourself,
In the same way you fall in love with another.
Unconditionally loving,
All the parts of yourself
That the light may have never touched.
Embracing all of you,
With love and acceptance.

For in the ever-evolving thralls of time
And the ever-fluctuating relationships,
Situationships,
Friendships,
And connections,
We are the one relationship,
The one connection,
In which we can never escape.

We must date ourselves,
To find ourselves.
This is how we truly learn
To love unconditionally.

Love For Self

I know that one of my greatest lessons in this life is to love myself unconditionally. Having spent most of my life hating myself, this has proven to be one of my hardest lessons to learn.

I remember back in 2019, after leaving my second abusive marriage, I desperately wanted to love all that I was. But I didn't know how. I didn't know where to begin. I tried everything I could think of. Meditating, journaling, crying, writing. I turned to tarot cards, oracle cards, Shamanic spiritual journeying, and more. Yet the message was always the same: *You need to love yourself.*

It was infuriating!

One day, amidst my sobs of frustration, I cried out for clarity. And then, like a whisper on the wind, the answer came, a simple question that made everything clear.

How do you love another?

From that moment on, things began to shift. I realized I needed to get to know myself, take myself on dates, spoil myself, extend grace to myself, and give myself the love I freely gave to others. I had to pour into myself in the same way I poured into those I loved. I had to get to know who I am and what I am passionate about. I had to get to know all the parts that I hid away. I had to start getting to know everything about me. The good, the beautiful, the seemingly bad and ugly. I had to get to know it all.

Some Questions For You:

- Do you have unconditional love for yourself?
- How much time do you give to yourself?
- Do you treat yourself the same way you want others to treat you?
- Do you give yourself the same love that you give to others?

Growth Through Love

The snow danced across the road
Like a blanket of frozen water on the wind,
Reminding me that even on the coldest days,
Nature embraces us the best way it knows how.
On these Winter days of hibernation,
I have found warmth,
Solace,
Love,
Home.
Entering a new mindset of growth through love,
Instead of growth through pain,
I am greeted with an inner peace
That words cannot fully elucidate.
With most things,
Our language falls short of portraying the beauty,
And madness,
Of our world,
Of our emotions.
Through these flickering pixels on a scrying mirror,
My emotions are flowing unprecedented.
A tsunami is forming within and all around me,
I am the master to which it ebbs or flows.
As I shift, the peace inside me expands,
I feel more feminine in these last few moments
Than I have in my entire journey here thus far.
This is no longer my journey of growth through pain.
This is now my journey of growth,
Through love.

Gentle Guidance

Throughout my life, I've learned my lessons through pain. Upon reflection, I've come to see how Divinity tries to guide me gently, with love. Yet, in my stubbornness, I dig in my heels, and the lessons become harsher and more painful.

I've had to realize there are other ways to learn what I need to understand. The more I embrace love, the more peace I feel. When things flow with love, my healing becomes easier.

Looking back on my upbringing, I can see where my belief in lessons being tied to pain comes from. My parents "taught" me through pain. My siblings and I endured intense physical and emotional abuse as a method of "guidance." This created a mindset where I felt I hadn't achieved anything unless pain was involved.

Now, I'm learning to embrace loving lessons, allowing Divinity to guide me with peace and love. My days of resistance and pain are behind me, and this shift is causing incredible things to unfold in my life.

Some Questions For You:

- Do you grow through love or pain?
- How did your parents teach you when you were young?

Breath Sleep

In to four,
Out to four.
My mind bustles
Like the busy streets of the city
It's 2am…
Thoughts zooming in and out
Energy pulsating from every direction.
In to five
Out to five.
Words pour from my subconscious
Into my mind
Screaming to be written down,
To be recorded.
I obey.
In to six,
Out to six.
I feel my body calm.
My mind slows.
Sleepiness hits my eyes.
They close.
In to seven,
Out to seven.
Sleep…..

From Anxiety to Peace

From the outside, you might think I'm a "perfectly normal" and functioning person. Yet, I've struggled with high-functioning anxiety my entire life. On the surface it may appear that I have everything together, but inside, it often feels like a war-zone—a constant state of anxiety and survival.

Over time, I've discovered tools that help me calm and center myself. Writing and deep breathing are two practices that ground me, bringing me back to the present moment. While I still carry a great deal of anxiety through life, these tools, along with strengthening my self-love and boundaries, have helped my anxieties slowly drift away.

But this anxiety still tends to rear its ugly head during moments of emotional/physical abuse or in chaotic social settings where booze flows and messy energy disrupts my peace. In those moments, I turn to journaling, breathing, and avoiding environments or people that amplify my anxiety. These practices help me cultivate inner peace, allowing me to rest and embrace a more serene existence on this planet.

This poem reflects those times when my mind wakes me in the middle of the night or early morning. When that happens, I honor my need to write. Breathing always helps ease me back into sleep, guiding me gently into rest.

SOME QUESTIONS FOR YOU:

- Anxiety is part of life and we all feel it at some point. How do you feel anxiety in your body?
- How do you ease your anxieties?
- What are your tools to get through anxious times?
- What is in your toolbelt for getting through these times? As an example do you journal or do breathing exercises like I do?

Early Mornings

It is the quiet part of my day,
The space of the day where my mind has not kicked into gear.
The time when my emotions are raw and exposed.
I feel heavy and deep today.
I feel all the masks I have worn,
All the watering down of myself so I am more acceptable…
I see the potential in others and fall for that.
I can clearly see that the same happens to me.
People fall for a version of me they think I am,
A version I never truly am.
This has a bitter sting for me today.
People love me at first,
And then that love fades as they get to know me.
Or maybe the love they have for themselves fades, I don't know.
Maybe my love intimidates,
Maybe what I see causes them to reflect and then hate.
Regardless, I know this,
Today my heart aches.
I feel like I am faced with rejection
At almost every turn these last few weeks,
Months,
Years.

Jobs, friends, lovers, projects stalled, businesses not working,
et cetera
et cetera
et cetera
I know the Universe has a plan,
But the energies that are fluxing and flowing
Have my heart feeling heavy and deep today.
They have me wanting to cry and scream to the heavens.
They have me wanting to run,
To fly
To flee.
But I will not.
I will sit with this.
I will feel it.
Today I will embrace the parts of myself
That I want to flee from.
Today I will say no to what does not resonate with who I am.
I will not say yes to anything that is less
Than what I need,
Want,
Deserve.
Today I will mourn,
So I can move on in a whole and healthy way.
Emotions are my early mornings.

Love Promise

I have never had an issue in seeing the good in people,
Seeing the potential of all they could be,
Seeing all their greatness right under all their pain.
No, I have never had that problem.

My problem lies in the fact that I fall in love
With the potential that people are not yet,
And may never step into.
I don't see the truth of people,
I don't want to.

As I sat with this mind-opening realization I found this:
It was the only way
I could survive my upbringing with love,
My soul chose to see the good,
See the potential,
In everyone, especially my abusers.

Without this my love would have died,
I would have been a completely different creature
Than the one I am today.

My blindness of how people truly were
Saved my love as a child,
But my blindness as an adult is killing it.

So, I will now make this promise
To that child within that saved my love:

I will continue to see the good, see the potential,
I will even help those who ask for it.
But my heart will never sway to this illusion again.
My love is strong and pure,
And will belong to the potential and good
That my future partner already possesses.

Breaking Free

There are parts of me that only I have seen,
Parts that pulse to a unique tone.
I have been formed from birth
To live in a manner that is befit
A good, Christian, civilized, woman.

But in my mind I have always beat to a different drum,
In my mind I am free to explore all I am.
As I write, I realize I am expressing
All of the deep desires,
Fantasies,
And ecstasies that have played through my mind
My entire life.
As this cage around me shatters, I choose freedom.

I don't want what you say I should want,
I want to flow to the energy of the music.
I want to get lost in the sensual and erotic energy of others.

I am so tired of the restrictions
That living in a civilized society
Has put on everyone,
Has put on me,
Has put on women.
I am tired of whining and excuses.
Blaming upbringings for bad behavior.
It's bullshit.

I feel everything.
I feel your energy,
My energy,
The energy of the earth,
I feel the energy of emotions,
I feel body language.
I feel it all.

When I feel something is off,
Or there is an issue,
I have to address it.
Work through it,
Heal it.
Communicate.

When I said
I wanted someone who could weather my storms,
I meant someone
Who could handle the expression of emotions.
Mine are powerful,
I am powerful.
And I am tired of watering myself down.

We cannot be happy
Or party all the time,
This is a toxic way of thinking and living.
Emotions are our guides
Our teachers
They tell us when we need to communicate,
When we need to rest,
Or when we need to set better boundaries.
What we "need" is to learn how
To communicate and listen more effectively.

I choose to break free,
I choose a different tribe,
a different energy.
I will no longer try to fit into this mold.
I am free
And no one
Will cage me ever again.

All I Have Is Me

Words used to flow through my fingers
Like honey on warm toast.
But they have become less
As I have traveled inward
To face the parts of myself that have been abused
By myself and others.

Over the years, I have let men take pieces of me…
I have allowed friends to invade my peace
Stomping on my boundaries for the sake of the friendship.

As I call all the pieces of myself back,
I realize that I have not been loved
In the way in which I love others.

When I close my eyes and focus on myself,
I feel such powerful love,
So powerful that it could conquer anything.

I finally have that love for myself.
It gives me power, strength, and magick.

Power to see that I need to be chosen and accepted for all I am.
Strength to stand for what I believe
and setting boundaries accordingly.
Magick to create the world I want for myself and my children.

I see how people just wanted parts of me,
The parts they deemed good and fun.
The parts that nurture and care.

But no one has yet to weather my storms,
To stick with me when my world is falling apart.
To not abuse or take advantage of all that I give,
And all that I am.

I am learning to be selfish
Learning to set boundaries.
Because at the end of the day
All I have is me.

Lessons From The Dirt

Her roots wind and twist,
Through the dark rich soil.
Her branches reach into the wide unknown,
Like roots planted in the sky.

Can I be rooted,
And still, have wings?
I now know how caged birds feel.
Wanting so badly to unfold into the heavens,
To feel the breeze lift and sway my existence
To a new and unknown place.

I pull when my emotions become too much.
I pull the long delicate strands of hair,
I pull weeds that fill my gardens.
I pull away,
I pull at the ones I love for answers,
For answers that never come.

I try and eliminate weeds in my life,
But they inevitably come back,
With a vengeance that is untameable.
This is the true wild fury of nature.

I can find peace in this life,
For brief moments.
But only if those in it
Can find peace and happiness as well.

I don't understand…
Why there is rarely peace here,
It seems to come and go
With the passing winds.

This is where I am now,
This is where I live.
Learning the lessons that need to be learned…
The same lessons,
Deeper lessons,
The spiral of the lesson.

The darker chapters that need to be embraced,
Not forgotten or pushed away.
For I am the dark and the light,
I am everything,
And I am nothing…

I have lived with my roots in the sky,
Found shelter in these branches.
Felt the sun on my flesh,
And the winds in my hair.

But now it is my time to live
With my roots in the ground.
Absorbing the nutrient-rich lessons.
To live with the dirt,
And all those that dwell upon and in it.

It isn't in my blood to give up,
Giving up is never an option.
But I will no longer fight,
I am tired of fighting.

It is a time of healing and learning.
A time of letting go.
A time of embracing my ever-changing,
True self.

Breathing Life

Life is the sun on my face through a passing window,
A hot cup of tea on an icy cold day,
Breath in my lungs,
Love in my heart.
I feel the glitter of goosebumps on my skin.
Every breath deeper and deeper,
My stress melts away.
And the heaviness falls,
Like the avalanche of snow off a mountainside.
Life is breathing into the seemingly simple
Pleasures of living.

Leaning Into Simple Pleasures

For those who struggle with anxiety and PTSD, as I do, it's essential to find ways every day to ease the soul. For me, this means cherishing the simple and magical parts of my life, and leaning into those brief but blissful moments that have the power to completely shift my outlook. Each of these miraculous moments holds the potential to bring peace and a new perspective.

Some Questions For You:

- What simple pleasures bring you peace?
- Can you add more of these moments to your everyday?

Choices

I have been away from the sun, the stars, the moon, the light.
The darkness that is a deep part of myself,
That I have run from,
Is now at the forefront of my mind.

Who is this darker being looking back at me
In the ripples of space and time?
The howl of the galaxy lingers in my bones,
And the abyss of blackness shines through my eyes.

What a choice, a choice to thrive, or a choice to survive?
Both are technically living, are they not?
Energetic formations spark patterns in my brain,
Is this 'Who I am?'

Are we not really just the choices we make?
Even if the choices feel 'wrong'
We are our choices…
I am choosing my darker side,
Perhaps for a time…

And perhaps not completely.
But I do feel the warm darkness comforting me,
While the light brings Winter.
Not completely delving into either light or dark,
A constant limbo in the gray.

Level scales creating chaos,
All Dark or all Light for balance and peace.
Choices, choices, choices,
All we really are,
And all we'll ever really be.

Lost You, Found Me

I am the fire,
Burning strong and true,
The wind kindles my flames.
I dance upon the water.

I am a fierce force of love and beauty,
Some cannot handle the pulse of my soul.
Honesty is my nature,
Even if it takes me time
To gain the courage to speak.

You may think you know me,
But you only know what you want to see.
I have made it further
And done more things from my dreams
Than most could obtain in one lifetime
Let alone the courage to even try.

But I won't let it stop me,
I am worth the stars and the moon,
The galaxies.
I am worth all the things
In this Universe and the next.

I'm done settling,
I'm done thinking that I am not
Worth all the great things that this life holds,
I will never stop living and experiencing.

I had to lose you,
To find me.
Lose you,
To fully grasp all that I deserve in this life.
Lose you,
So I could thrive.

Floating Sleep

She peered
Into the swirling cave of wonders
And found herself.
Ever so floating there
Among all that glittered and glowed.
Suspended
In an endless sleep.

Emotional Warrior

I no longer fear any of my emotions,
I welcome their storms.
I am not afraid to be engulfed by them,
To let them take me over.

For I know that I cannot get lost in the darkness,
For I am always exactly where I am.
I cannot become lost in anything
If I've already found myself.

So I will let these emotions take hold of me,
I will listen to what they are telling me.
I will listen to the lessons they are teaching me,
I will let their harshness soften me.

For there are some things in this life
We cannot change, we cannot fix.
Sometimes we have to sit with our loneliness
Have to sit with what we crave,
Whether that be connection with a lover,
Or a friend.

Sometimes we will not have the option,
For connection.
But these heavier emotions show us
What it is we truly desire,
And help us figure out what it is
We truly want in this life.

I've always felt like a warrior.
Not the kind of warrior that sheds blood,
Although I have felt this way at times,
But an emotional warrior.
My fight has always been through surrendering.

Forging Power

She could feel the world around her pressing in.
Like a vise slowly adding pressure to her chest.
Breathing became difficult.
Thoughts became clouded.
The anxiety crushing.
A quiet voice
Came from within her darkness
"Face me"
So she took a deep breath and stood tall,
A warrior,
A goddess,
A woman on a journey to heal herself.
She stood there and looked into the cool darkness.
Felt it all around her as she stepped into it.
This is shadow work, she thought.
This was her work,
Her medicine.
For everyone it is different,
For her, it was standing in her power,
Not as a warrior ready for battle,
But as a woman laying down her sword.
A white flag,
This is how she befriended her demons,
Within her shadows.

By standing tall with them,
Embracing them,
Calling them into her power.
For she would no longer be held as a victim,
Not ever again.
Nor would she bloody herself
In a fight that would make the vice grip her more tightly.
No, this was about sweet surrender.
A warrior's surrender,
To herself.
An awakening of a power so immense
She radiated it through her whole world.
Those who wished her ill stayed away,
Those who needed her protection
Found solace under her wings.
But she would not let them stay there.
For they could not.
Instead, she helped them fully stand
As their own warrior selves.
And through her strength,
She forged an army of warriors
That stood tall with their shadows as their guides.
She forged a mighty power from the dark.
And helped bring balance
To this chaotic world.

Our Dark Parts

If you could see all the dark parts of me,
All the pieces that are frayed and sharp,
All the pieces that are bruised and rotting.
If you could see all those pieces at once,
Would you still love me unconditionally?
Would I still shine like a bright star?
Would I still amaze you?

Or would my darkness cause fear within you?
Would it cause you to run?
Would my darkness challenge your ego?

What I realize is that love is only beautiful
When you can still love
After seeing the darkness within someone
Where you've only ever seen magick.

But there is magick in the darkness as well,
For those unafraid to step into it.
I challenge you to see your own darkness
Especially when it is reflected to you from another.

Recognizing Light and Dark

I went through a phase where I felt I could only be loved in parts. When I turned 40, I began reflecting on what I truly wanted in friendships and with a partner. That year became a turning point—a "hell year" of 'fuck no's!' Through this rejecting of toxic people, my life began filling with souls who matched my energy and vibrated on my wavelength.

I moved from a space where I attracted people who initially loved me to people who saw all of me and found only magick. I stepped away from people who tried to shun or control me the moment I expressed emotions beyond being fun and agreeable. While there were times I stayed longer than I should have, it became easier and easier to burn those bridges.

At the same time, this process fueled my anger—anger at how people treated me and others. That anger, however, became a tool for reflection. It showed me my own toxic behaviors, the areas within myself, that needed to shift and change. I think a huge lesson in this life is realizing that we are all toxic and manipulative at times. It is what you do after that matters. You must reflect and get to the root of 'why?'. I always tell my kids that sorry means nothing without changed behavior. That same rule goes for everyone.

Some Questions For You:

- What is it in others that really upsets you?
- Can you reflect and see if you too may hold some of those toxic traits?
- If you do, can you listen to what you need and give yourself love and grace so you can heal?
- We all have light and dark (or heavy and light) within us. What is your light? What is your dark?

Maturing

I saw a quote that said,
Maturity is not forcing people to choose you.
This hit an unhealed part of me.

I have always tried to convince
The wrong people to stay,
I have always convinced
Myself to stay,
When all I wanted
Was to choose something different.

I am not the friend that people think of,
For fun times.
I bring rich intensity,
I challenge people to think deeply,
And be the best version of themselves.

I am done chasing people.
Friends, lovers, family.
I show up for people when they need me.

But I will no longer stress,
When someone decides to not call,
To not communicate,
To not show up.

I will keep moving,
I will keep flowing,
I will keep growing.
I will keep maturing.

ReInventing

I keep thinking about reinventing myself,
Or maybe it's more of a coming back,
To who I truly am,
Or a discovering of who I truly am.

I've always allowed myself,
To be versions that other people would find palatable.
I would create versions of myself,
That might make people like me.

All these versions were me,
But they were just pieces of me.
The darker, more intense, more risqué pieces of myself,
I've always hidden away.

I have never fully been who I feel myself to be.
I've only ever been watered down versions of who I am.
It's true I am caring, I am sweet,
I am the quenching rain after a deep drought.

But I am also a hurricane,
A hot, burning, wild fire,
I will challenge every viewpoint and value
That you hold to be true.

I will not allow people to become stagnant,
I will always push them to grow,
And encourage them to sit with their uncomfortable feelings.
To get to know who they are,
And to forge their own path.

I am a deeply loyal friend and lover.
But I also know when to walk away.
Part of me feels like I'm 20 again,
Trying to discover, rediscover, reclaim who I am.

20 but with the maturity from all the heartaches,
All the lessons.
This new phase in my life,
Is that of deep love, firm boundaries,
And the determination to always be myself.

I know that someday
The right people will cross my path,
But until that happens,
I will sit with this longing
As I ReInvent and ReFind myself.

My Plate

I hold my head high
As things slowly pile upon me
One by one adding weight
Adding worry
Adding stress
One by one creating a heaviness
That is difficult to hold.
I feel my life changing
Shifting
Like the sands that are blown in a desert
By the ever passing winds.
I long for a simple life
A peaceful life.
I am tired
And want nothing more
Than to escape
To a cabin in the woods
And to live alone in peace

To spend my days
Writing
Creating
Loving
Living

Goodbye Mother

I have blocked you
In every way I could,
But the voicemail's still come through.
I feel like a bad child
Whenever I hear your voice,
Even now,
After all this healing,
After all the work I have done.

Your voice triggers a part of me
That feels wrong for existing,
But I do not call you back,
And for a short time,
I live with that feeling of
Wrongness,
That feeling of being a bad child,
That feeling of being a bad person.

Even though I know
I will never speak to you again,
I still feel pain for you,
I still empathize,
I still feel your sadness.
But I cannot live
A healthy life
With you in it.

Goodbye, Mother.

Cutting Out a Parent

How does one even begin to explain their reasoning?

I do not have a single kind or fond memory of my mother. For years, I tried to build a relationship with her as an adult, but every time I heard her voice, it felt like I shouldn't exist. No matter what I did, I always felt wrong in everything I did.

There is no remorse from her for the things she did to my siblings and I. She genuinely believes she was an amazing mother. She has even fabricated stories of events that never happened and clings to them as if they were real. Perhaps she cannot face the terrible things she, and our stepfather, did to us.

Whatever her reason, I had to say goodbye. For it was the only way I could begin to heal and flourish. But this is no easy road. She still calls and even though she is blocked, I still listen to the voicemail's. I hear the sorrow in her voice. I don't know why I do it to myself, but for those few moments I feel the sorrow of what cutting her out is doing to her and to me. She sounds like a scared lost woman full of sorrow and pain.

For me, this is a wound that will never heal, and only those who have had to cut out a toxic/abusive parent can understand, but I hope my explanation can shine even the slightest light on what it feels like.

Some Questions For You:

- Is there anyone in your life that makes you feel less?
- What does your parents voice trigger within you? Happiness? Love? Fear? Safety? etc...
- What would your life look and feel like if you cut out the people that make you feel less than you are?

My Father

During the quiet pieces of the day,
You whisper to me,
The sweet lullabies
You were robbed of telling.
The world was not kind to you.
You were not kind to yourself.
Your heart was the biggest I had ever seen,
And ever will.
In spite of all your pain,
And sorrow,
You gave without thought,
Without quarry,
Without want.
You would give until your back broke,
Your hands bled,
And then you'd give more.
I can't tell you how my heart is breaking,
How it cracks seeing your face on my phone,
But I can't call.
I can never call again.
I can never hear you again.
I can never see you in this life again.
I am sorry we were robbed of so much time,
By the hands of evildoers,
And by the feet of my wandering spirit.
I'm sorry I left you,
I'm sorry I wasn't there.
I love you with all my soul.

My Father: A Broken Man

I met my father when I was 25 and stayed with him for a couple of years when I was 29. During those two years, I got to know who he was, what he had been through, and my family on his side. I remember feeling an intense anger toward him—for not fighting harder to keep us away from my mother and stepfather. I was angry that he had allowed us to live a life of abuse, separated from all the love I experienced during those short two years.

My mother took us away when I was about four. My father spent the next 21 years living in his own personal hell, not knowing if we were alive, not knowing if we were okay, and unaware of what our mother and stepfather were doing to us.

As a mother myself, I can't imagine the daily torment of not knowing if my children were safe or if they were living in a nightmare. A part of me would die every single day from the unknowing.

I wrote this poem after my father passed away in 2018.

Some Questions For You:

- What kind of people are/were your parents?
- What kind of trauma did they endure in their own lives?
- What impact did they leave on your life?

US
1
East Coast
Greenway

To My Son

I am sorry I had you so young,
During a time in my life when I hated myself.
I have loved you more
Than I've ever loved any being on this planet,
And that love saved me.

I am sorry I couldn't show you how to love yourself,
I'm sorry I couldn't show you
How to take care of yourself properly.
You got a version of me that was unhealed,
A version that was deeply wounded.

Your sister has a version of me that is strong,
A version of me that has put in the work to heal,
A version of me that is not running.
I am sorry if the way I ran from life hurt you.

I never wanted you to have to live my life,
Live the pains I had to suffer.
Life will not be easy for you,
Just as it has never been easy for me.

I am sorry you are hurting,
I am sorry I couldn't give to you
The tools that I'm giving your sister.
But I want you to know this;
You can conquer anything,
And you are loved so deeply.

Loved not just because you are my son,
But because your light shines so brightly
It lights up the Universe.
I hope that you can start seeing your light,
Seeing your brilliance.

I will always be here for you,
My beautiful son.

To My Daughter

I am sorry you had to endure
The same traumas I had to endure.
I wish I could say that
This life would be easy for you.
I wish I could say that the traumas
Will not affect you.
But I can already see
How it has changed you.
I can already see your distrust of everyone,
Including yourself.
I can sense your fears
I can see your anger
I can feel why you need control.
You were told
That your voice was not true
You were taught that what you experienced
Was a joke.
Taught this by a person you trust
A person you just want to love you.
I am sorry that you think
The truth will cause you
To lose everything.
I am sorry that you only feel safe now
By lying about everything.
I hope you let your traumas in this life
Make you soft,
But strong,
And most of all I hope they teach you
To always choose you,
And to stand up for what is good,
Kind,
And right.
I know that you will grow up to be an amazing woman.
Until that time comes I hope you can fall into
Living your best childhood life.

The Silence Night Brings

The night, it serves as a reminder
That I am alone.
There is an emptiness within my soul,
A need
To be touched,
To be loved.

I need another bird to soar the ever-changing winds,
A companion to brave the rough seas,
A lover to explore the depths of the earth.
A partner in life,
A nurturer of my soul,
And keeper of my heart.

I love the night, for the quiet calm.
The silence that soothes my tired mind.
It brings me clarity on emotions and actions
That took place throughout the hurricane of the day.

A woman is not meant to be a single mother.
To be both the mother and the provider.
It is impossible to be both fully.
And so here I reside,
In a chaotic limbo between the two.

A Passing Phase

These late nights and tiring days have me feeling emotional,
Vulnerable,
More times than not I feel like I am a passing phase for people.
Something they want,
They need,
Or they crave,
Until they have me and then they are done.
My ego wants to be wanted,
But I have a deeper want in my soul to be valued.
I have never been truly valued.
I will give,
Call,
Reach out,
Until I realize
I am the only one initiating
So I disappear.
I truly don't understand people,
So selfish and stupid.
"Enlightened" Neanderthals
Stomping through a forest,
Killing everything.
I am not tired of giving myself to people,
I am tired of feeling alone when I do.
I have a love so deep and vast it cannot be contained.
A Love I want to share,
But I am just a passing phase.

Searching For Demons

I made a profound realization
About myself this morning.
As I do see the potential
And the light in people,
I also see their darkness.
I see their demons,
And that is what I am attracted to.
This energy is like a drug to me.
It brings out a part of me that I suppress,
A part of me that craves to be awakened.
With this comes me pouring into people,
Who do not pour back into me.
I am realizing that what I want is
To have someone fall in love with my darkness,
Someone who sees me,
And wants to be swallowed up with me.
Both of us
Swimming in the dark waters together.
Two demons
Forging new paths of connection,
Together.

Drawn to Darkness

I was trying to understand why I was always drawn to people who were abusive and toxic. This led me down a rabbit hole into the darker sides of myself, where I realized how deeply I craved someone who could truly understand, love, and accept me in all my facets—light and dark. Someone who wouldn't want to change me in any way.

This journey also revealed my lack of boundaries in what I give to people. I gave everything right away, pouring myself into others, only to reach a point of emptiness because I wasn't being poured into in the same way.

This poem was my realization that I was more drawn to someone's darkness, than to their light and potential.

SOME QUESTIONS FOR YOU:

- What are your darker sides?
- If you showed all of your darker sides who in your life would stand beside you and love you in your entirety?

To Be Touched

I need touch
Not in a
Sexual way
But in a connection
Sort of way

I need to feel your
Arms around me
In public
In private

I need us both
To be able to
Massage each other
To learn the dips
And curves,
To help our bodies heal
And to learn
Every inch of each other

I need to feel your
Arm around me
Your hand caressing my back
Whenever we are together

I need you to reach
For my hand
Caress my arms
Play with my hair

Because you love touching me
Because being away from me
Is torture
Because not touching me
Is just not an option

I need to be grabbed
Teased
And nurtured

I need to feel
Your energy
Dancing with mine
I need touch
To quench my soul

Without this kind of touch
I starve
I become a version of myself
That thinks there
Is something wrong with
Who I am

Because
In my mind
The denial of touch
Is a punishment.

Eyes Open, Eyes Closed

Eyes Open,
Eyes closed.
As I walk through this life.
My heart,
A vast trove that spills like the oceans
Upon a rocky beach.
Bubbly waters
Finding there way
Into every orifice of the earth that it touches.
When I give my love,
I give it completely.
With a fierceness that is untouchable.
But not unbreakable.
So if my love I have given to you,
My heart in your hands,
Hold it with care.
It can take a lot before it breaks,
But it needs no more scars upon its bleeding flesh.
And if I have fallen out of your love,
Do not try to let me down gently.
Push the sword right through and pull it out.
My blood will spill,
But like a Phoenix,
I will be reborn from my pain.

SOUL LOVE

I've opened my heart
To empty lovers,
Pouring my soul into them.
They consumed me
Like a fountain of youth.
My power
Empowering them,
My light
Healing them.

But I was not
Worth their love in return.
They wanted what I had to give,
Feeling they deserved it.

But this has never stopped me
From searching for the man
I knew was out there somewhere,
The man who
Was also searching for me.

No love is ever perfect,
Nor easy,
But I now realize how important it is
To find a partner who loves
In the ways in which I also love,
A love that is balanced
And poured into by both.

A love that takes its time
To know me deeply,
To know the depths of all that I am,
A slow down,
Deep soul loving,
Kind of love.

Finding Love

I have always found writing about melancholy and yearning to be easier than writing about joy and love. This is one of my first attempts to delve into this realm of writing without sounding too cheesy.

One of my greatest wishes of my heart is to find someone who loves me for exactly who I am, in all my entirety, loves me deep down to my soul. I realized not too long ago that I had been searching for this kind of love my whole life. It wasn't until I started loving myself that the Universe started testing me with partners. I went through dating hell and it beat my heart to a pulp. But that beating did nothing but soften me more; it created an energy within me every time I walked away from someone who wasn't right. That energy emanated my own pure love, like a beacon that was calling out to my person out there in the world.

Describing love and joy in a way that will closely echo its essence is a hard feat. I have never known a love like this before. I can't claim that it will last the test of time; my life has been full of too much change and heartache, too much trauma, for me to believe that this will last until my last breath on this planet. But I cherish what we have and what we are creating. This is a deep, healing kind of love. One that transcends any dream I could imagine.

<u>Some Questions For You:</u>

- What is a dream that your heart yearns for?
- If you are connected with someone, what does your love look like? Is it the kind of love that fills you?
- If you are not connected to anyone, what kind of love would pull you out of the single life?

An Evening Truth

The truth is that I miss you,
More than I will ever be able to admit.
My heart aches.
I am happy but I am also full of deep sorrow.

I try to do things to move on,
Move past,
But right now I am in a stage of mourning.

I don't know how long it will take,
It may take days, weeks, months,
Or even years.

The feeling is similar to when a loved one passes.
How do you keep living when the love you had is now dead?

I know I will keep living,
I know I will thrive,
I know I will eventually move on.

Perhaps it is the idea of love that I am mourning.
I feel part of my soul giving up on the very idea of it all together.

I have created a vision of the man that I want,
All the traits I want in a partner
A perfect man so I will never have to fall in love again.

Right now no one fits the bill,
And quite possibly never will.
I will stay in my solitude
Because I know I am worth nothing less.

I will mend this heart
Becoming strong in who I am,
Alone.

The Game of Love

Waking again at an ungodly hour,
I made the decision
That I would no longer look back.
I would smile in gratitude,
Looking only forward.

I decided I would no longer
Look up old lovers,
Just to see how they were.
I set myself free instead.

Through this,
I realized,
How much my heart is hurting,
How scared I am.
How much I truly wish
For a fairy-tale romance,
One that will last until I leave this world.

I realized how terrified I am,
Of getting hurt again.
My heart torn up,
In an endless loop.

This is the price
Of playing the game of love,
is it not?

Honestly,
I am not sure
That I want to play anymore.

I have so much to be thankful for,
But I feel a wall around my heart,
And I don't know that it can be taken down.

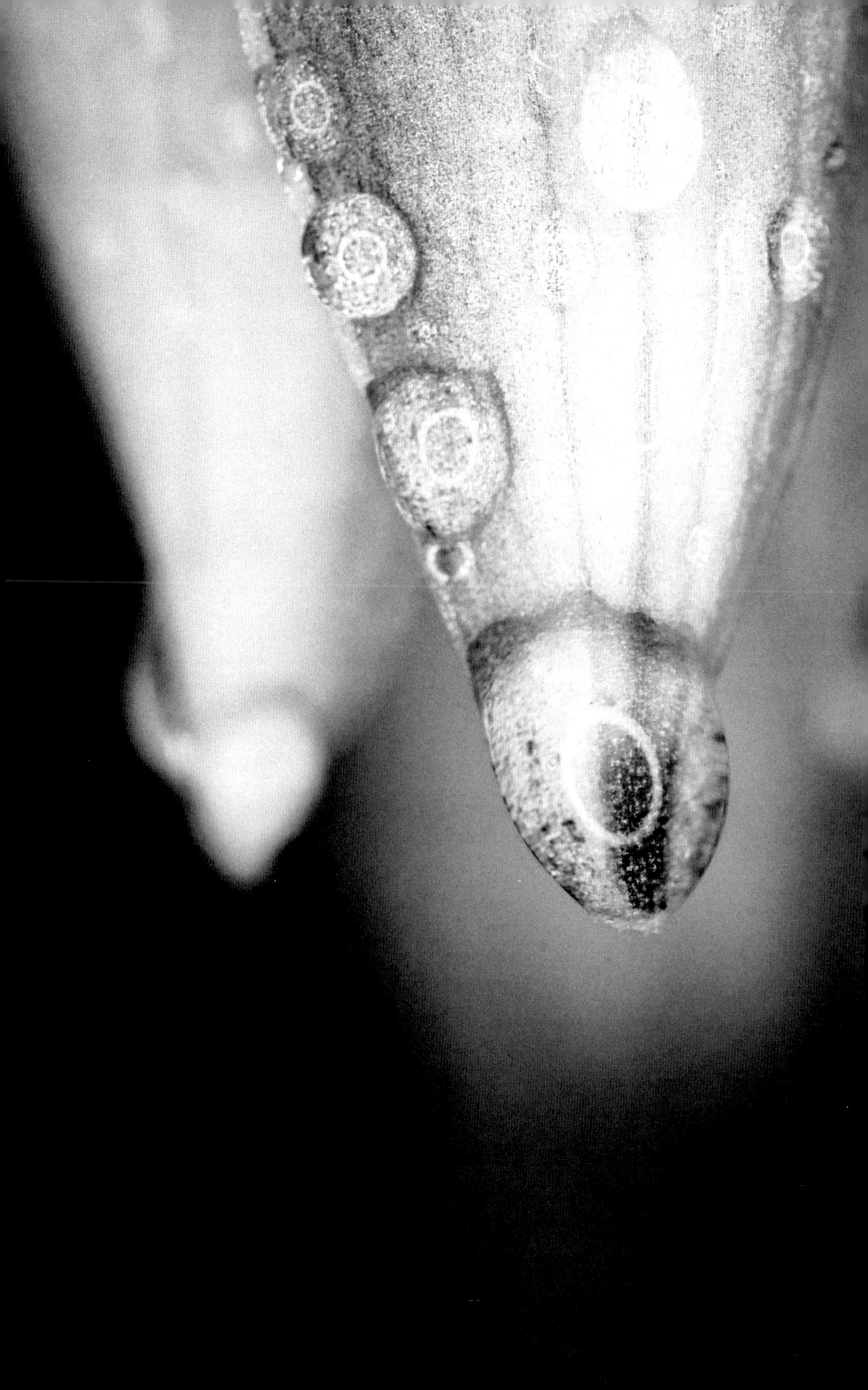

Divine Love

The stars shine
Brightly within your soul.
Escaping as flecks
Of glitter in your eyes.
Your spirit fills me,
Soothes me,
Allows me to ease into
All it means to be a woman.

Your love is healing.
Healing all the parts
That have scars, left by others.
Giving me a peace
That brings me closer
To Divinity.

THE BEAUTY OF LOVE

Love has a miraculous way of helping us heal and bringing us closer to the Divine, closer to spirit, closer to ourselves. At the beginning of most relationships, this love is felt intensely. It is both healing and transformative, splitting us open to feel things on a deeper level. Some people shine more brightly than others, and some have the power to heal parts of us we didn't even realize needed healing.

I feel that one of my soul's purposes is to let love heal me and to fully embrace it.

One of the lessons I've learned from opening my heart to others is that some people come into our lives to show us what we desire in love, even if they cannot sustain the act they present. In such cases, it's important to reflect on what we loved, recognize manipulation if it's present, and be willing to step away.

In the beginning of a relationship, the love we see from others is a reflection of how we ourselves love.

Some Questions For You:

- How does the love in your life make you feel?
- How does it make you feel on a spiritual level?
- Do you feel these same feeling when you are alone?
- If you are not in a relationship, what kind of love are you seeking? Or, what kind of love would make you want to exit the single life?

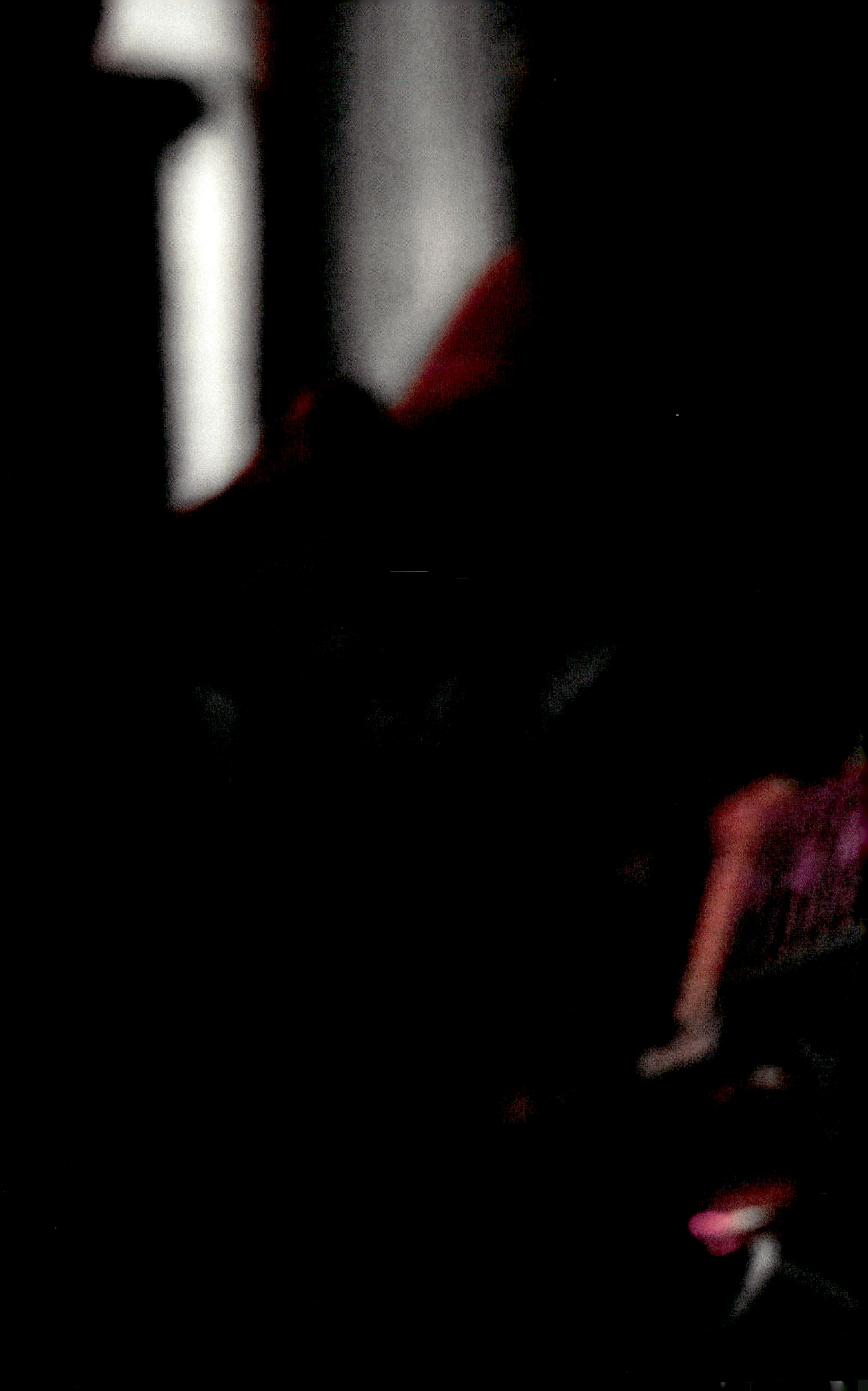

You

You,
Are the moonlight that kissed my soul
As I sat in my darkness.
Your presence,
A beacon that soothes me in my storms
And lulls me in my calm waters.
You're
The beat that has pulled my dreams ashore,
From the abyss of my being.
You,
Draw everything I embody
To the warm sandy beaches of our reality.
You've,
Made it safe to be all that I am,
To be all that I embody.
To say "I love you" will never be enough,
For you are my moon and stars,
My light in every dark corner,
My best friend,
And my greatest love.

Amour,
ardor,
resplendent,
original,
nourishing.

Aaron

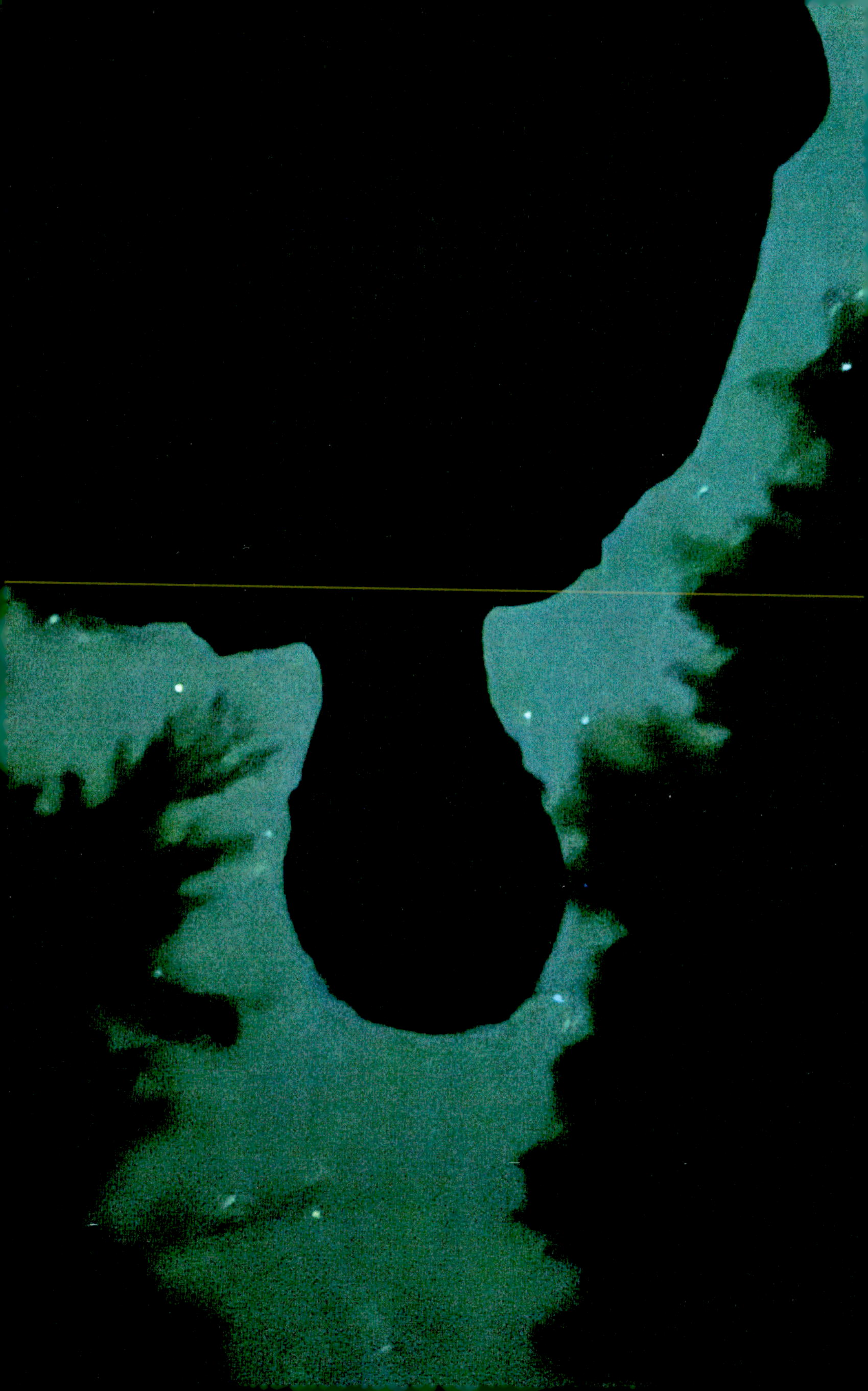

Humankind's Legacy

The dew it settles, on this dirty city,
But it does not wash away.
A cool rain temporarily cleanses away the filth,
But will never return it to the pristine of nature.

He says that he is for the betterment of our world,
And yet, only destruction lies in his path.
Experiments at the scientists' hands hurt before they heal.
What kind of world are we creating?

A prison of rules and regulations,
No one is free.
No one is free on a planet that we were all born upon,
On a planet that
Belongs to no one.

Do you see that forest over there?
Never mind, it now sits in your living room
For all to gawk and stare.

I see the world from an outside view.
There is most definitely a sickness in the mind of man.
Denying it only holds it true,
Admitting it frees you from its shackles,
And shows you the truth.

Do you remember the Passenger Pigeon?
The last one died in a zoo in 1914.
One guess as to how their extinction was brought about.

Humans are a plague upon this planet.
We reproduce and multiply
Like roaches, rats, flies

If children are something you desire,
Why do you want them?
I assure you they are all for selfish reasons.
We are the weeds upon the planet.
We treat our world like we have another one to go to.

I would gladly lay down my life
For the survival of another species.
Would you?

We destroy and we consume,
For our pleasure's sake,
For our laziness' sake.
If we stop our consuming today, all of us, everyone,
Would we be able to clean our planet?

Do you know where your non-recyclable trash goes?
I do...
To a landfill in India...

A wise man once told me,
"We can never kill our planet.
But we can make it so we cannot live upon it,
Cannot survive in its air,
Cannot live on its ground,
Cannot breathe its air."
I would sadly agree.

The planet will continue spinning after we have all died away.
Maybe the planet will do the "dirty" work for us,
Maybe another ice age,
Or disease,
Will come our way and hit the reset button on our planet.

So, let's just keep on doing what we are doing
And wait for some other force to fix all of our problems.

We Live In Dead Trees

I have always found it strange that we cut down the trees,
To only live in their corpses.

As I watch the birds scatter the lawn
My thoughts drifted to their lives during a storm.
Safe in their nests
Within the protection of the tree.

Why do we live in boxes of dead trees?
Why do we not live
With the birds inside the canopy?

As I type,
From within my own box of dead trees,
I ponder
The different ways to habitate this planet.

I have never really liked houses,
Too easy for me to hibernate
And never come out.

I would love to live in a tree-house.
Like a big nest suspended in the trees
Instead of a coffin, on the ground.

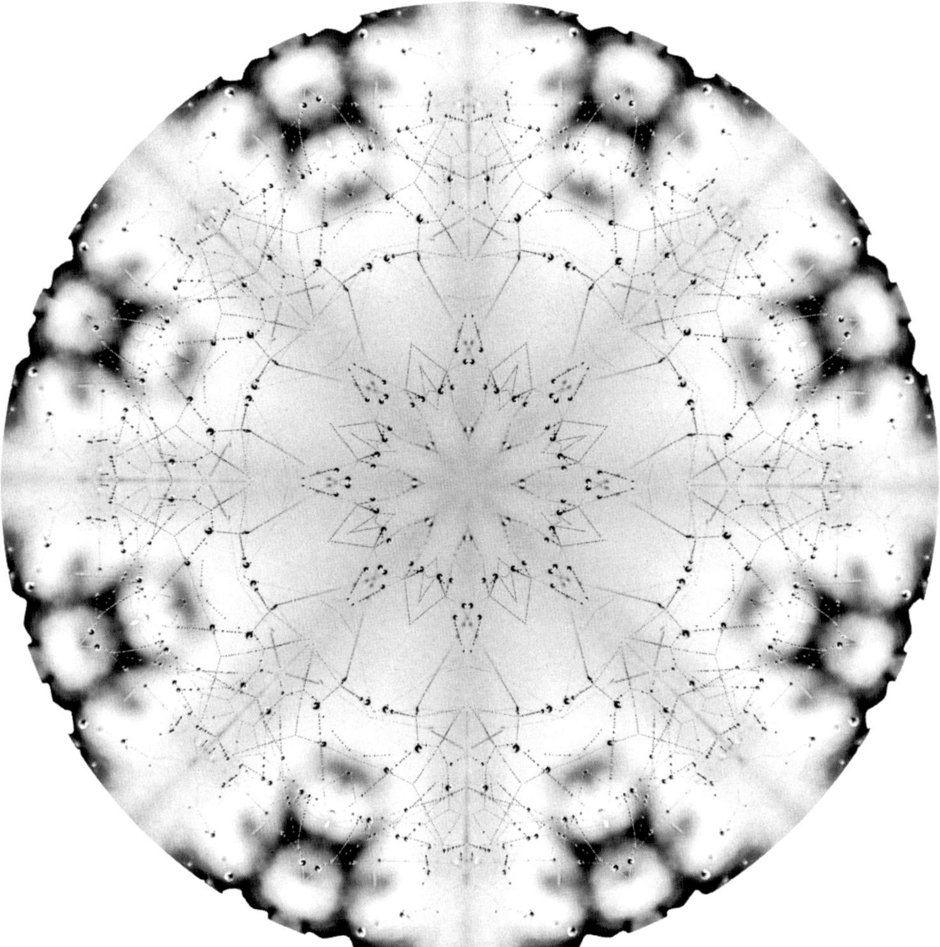

Superficial Conversations

Superficial conversations are difficult for me,
They bore me.
Sometimes, I feel too rich,
Like a dessert
That is only an occasional indulgence.

If I ask you how your day is going,
I am looking for a rich and deep response.
I am looking for you to shed your layers,
Shed your tears,
Share your joys.

Life is too short for simple interactions
That will only be forgotten
And carried away with the passing winds.

Rich interactions are remembered,
They are savored,
They take a place within our minds,
And within our souls

I see people in this park interacting on superficial levels.
I can see them,
Each just waiting for the other to stop talking
So they can speak their meaninglessness
For all to hear.

There is no listening,
There is no pure connection,
Just their obnoxious noise
Filling up this air.

Never Lose Your Words

Words have always been a part of my soul,
A part of my rich inner worlds.

They flow and flex in my mind like the changing tides.
An emotional ocean of hurricanes and calm waters,
And everything in between.

I love sharing these parts of myself,
Connection is something that must be strived for,
Especially in these trying screened times.

We must never lose our words,
Our ways to connect to each other,
Our ability to weave
Stories and emotions into beautiful tapestries,
Using only our words.
No, this should never be lost.

I give this small warning,
A truth, if you will,
If you let technology speak for you,
You will lose your humanity,
You will lose connection,
And ultimately become the screen you stare into.

Never lose your words and always speak your truths.

Lost At The River

Give me a river winding through the trees any day,
With nature fluttering around,
Energy moving and flowing,
It is a life force.

Lakes and oceans are beautiful but I do not find peace within them,
I do not find solace.
They cannot stand to the raging beauty of a river.

The majestic, loud, and vibrant power, of a river.
Perhaps it is the continual forward flow that I resonate with so deeply.
The water creates a deafening sound
That drowns out everything in my mind.

Rivers are my serenity,
Forging their own path when life has them swelling,
Flowing through and over any obstacles with grace and power.

Rivers in the forest also allow me to enjoy the sun from a shady place,
Without the bite of the heat upon my cheeks and nose.
I could sit and be lost here forever.

My True Freedom

I saw a hawk soaring the pastel blue sky,
The clouds like pillows for when he decided to rest his wings.
My heart wanted to fly out of my chest
To soar the heavens alongside him;
A spirit on the winds, unbridled and free.
Maybe it's that I have a traveler's spirit,
Or that I understand something that many have forgotten.

As I sit here on this fluffy, seemingly comfortable, couch,
All I want is a seat that is of a tree and grass.
I want the wind to dance and play in my hair,
The sounds of crickets and toads in my ears at night.
When I look up into the dark sky,
I want to see the moon and stars fill the sky
From horizon to horizon.

There is a freedom outside of these walls
That we have become so comfortable to call home.
Home is the grass and mud under my feet,
The sweet melody of a river,
And gaze of a mountain,
A sunset over a valley of flora and fauna
Untouched by man's inventions.

I am more often than not pulled to these places,
A pull that is so deep that when I do follow
I meld and feel my connection
to everything in this universe.

What keeps me in these prisons
Of metal and sheet-rock?
I feel so disconnected from what is truly important.
I fill my time with nonsense;
Occupying myself
Until complete exhaustion,
Then starting all over.

What drives us to live in this way?
Like we're on a freight train
With no certain destination,
Plowing through everything that is around us to
enjoy.
What prize is there at the end of the track?
I can't imagine it is a very fulfilling one.

I'd be willing to bet
That you'd feel emptier than when you started.
There is nothing ever to be gained,
Only enjoyed.
And through the enjoyment,
We find freedom and peace.

I suppose we all find our enjoyment
In different places,
Mine just happen to live in the ebb and flow
Of everything that is found outside
The walls and devices
We become so lost inside.

Listen

I hear the world through more than my ears,
I listen with my body and soul.
Sounds reverberate and vibrate through me,
Like a tuning fork
Preparing me for the incoming energy.

The pulse in my chest, the rhythm of music,
They reach deep inside, stirring my energy.
In nature, did you know trees talk?
The wind whispers through the leaves,
The trees echo back potent energy.

I place my hands on the bark, I feel
The immense wisdom and energy,
More than the tree can physically hold.
When I truly want to see something,
I close my eyes, open myself,
And dance in the energy of what I "see" there.

People, animals, reptiles,
Everything we see and cannot see,
They all have energy and vibration.
So, I say:

Listen to the world with something other than your ears,
See beyond just your eyes,
Feel deeper than your skin,
And love with every part of your being.

Tune in, vibrate, reciprocate,
In the energy that unites us all,
That pulses through everything we know.
Listen

A Chasing Phase

So long I have chased the past,
Through tangling vines and thorns,
To find myself pained and scarred.
Bleeding all over my present.

What once was,
And people I once ran to,
Are no more.
There is no solace in their words or company,
Only empty versions of who we once were.

The wind blows so fiercely here
Telling us to move with it,
Not to stay.
I used to look to past flames,
Search them out.

Strings holding me
To an idea of who I once was,
And what I once wanted.
But no more.

Depression, anxiety, anger,
Is what lies for us
When we try to catch our past fireflies
Fleeing in the night.

We are who we are in this very moment,
No past echo of who we were will ever be again.
Our future selves are unwritten upon the pages of life,
We are blank canvases.

We choose who we are,
Who we will be.
The lessons we learn show us who we want to be,
And who we don't want to be.

We grow, we change, we evolve.
This is who we truly are,
Evolutionary Beings, Constantly changing.

Rainy Roads

I love driving on the roads in silence,
Especially after a day of rain.

The sound of the wheels,
Grabbing the road,
The water splashing up around the edges.

The gentle hum of the engine,
And the beautiful Maine terrain.
The feeling of every crack,
Fissure,
And hole in the road.

Reminding me
That even though the road may be bumpy,
It still gives way to where I am going.

Driving through the silence,
The road becomes a metaphor
For life's journey.
Sometimes bumpy,
Yet always leading somewhere.
Even if the destinations unknown.

A journey that is embraced
With each turn of the wheel.

The Dead Tree

There's a dead tree in my yard that I resonate with,
Rooted deep in the earth,
Seemingly dead to any human who may gaze upon her.
But as she stands tall,
Her branches slowly falling to the earth,
One by one,
She gives life,
Even in her death.

Within her,
Beneath the peeling bark,
And between her splitting layers,
Bugs call home,
And in her once lush canopy,
She feeds the birds,
And gives them a place to rest their wings.
She is still very much alive,
Caring for and nurturing the world around her.
I can feel her soul still within her core.
She emanates a glow of life.

She is like a wise old crone,
Still nurturing,
Still teaching,
Still living.
She may seem dead to any human passing by,
But to me,
I see her life.
I see her as still living.

I resonate with this tree
Because people all too often make assumptions
Based on what they see.
No one takes the time to really look at someone,
Or something,
To see how their soul shines.

I'm a soul see'er.
People come and go from my life on a constant basis.
I'm just as this tree,
Standing tall,
Rooted in the earth,
Caring for those who pass through.

I don't truly feel seen by most.
Not many know me on a soul level,
Just as not many will see this tree
As anything other than a dead tree.

May You Find Yourself, and Love ALL You Are

Made in the USA
Columbia, SC
04 April 2025

a5feb24a-f644-4ab2-b462-53cfeaa33b06R04